Renewing Marital Intimacy

....

Closing the Gap Between
You and Your Spouse

David Powlison

New Growth Press
www.newgrowthpress.com

All Scripture quotations, unless otherwise indicated, are taken from the *Holy Bible,* New International Version®, NIV®. Copyright © 1973, 1978, 1984 by International Bible Society. Used by permission of Zondervan. All rights reserved.

New Growth Press, Greensboro, NC 27404
Copyright © 2008 by Christian Counseling & Educational Foundation. All rights reserved. Published 2008

Cover Design: The DesignWorks Group, Nate Salciccioli and Jeff Miller, www.thedesignworksgroup.com

Typesetting: Robin Black, www.blackbirdcreative.biz

ISBN-10: 1-934885-34-7
ISBN-13: 978-1-934885-34-5

Library of Congress Cataloging-in-Publication Data

Powlison, David, 1953-
 Renewing marital intimacy : closing the gap between you and your spouse / David Powlison.
   p. cm.
 Includes bibliographical references and index.
 ISBN 978-1-934885-34-5
 1. Marriage—Religious aspects—Christianity. 2. Intimacy (Psychology)—Religious aspects—Christianity. I. Title.
 BV835.P69 2008
 248.8'44—dc22
                                        2008011925
Printed in Canada
21 20 19 18 17 16 15 14   8 9 10 11 12

You started out telling each other everything. Time flew by when you were together. You listened intently when 1 Corinthians 13 was read at your wedding. "Love is patient, love is kind. It does not envy…" you nodded your head. It all seemed so easy then.

But now you have nothing to say to each other. The intimacy and trust you once enjoyed are gone—replaced by bickering, long silences, and hurried conversations about your schedules.

Why Do Marriages Become Distant?

Marriage is the most intimate of relationships. When a man and woman marry, they are meant to be one in heart and mind. God calls this being "one flesh." Why do two people who have pledged to be faithful, kind, and loving to one another become separate?

Long ago in the Garden of Eden, Adam and Eve enjoyed perfect intimacy with God and with each other. But when they disobeyed God, their intimate relationship with him and with each other was destroyed. When you think about it, you'll notice that the way you treat your spouse reflects the way you treat God. The same things that cause distance in your relationship with God cause distance in your relationship with your spouse.

Jesus told a parable that gives a graphic picture of what creates distance in our relationship with God and one another. According to Jesus, it's what's in your heart that makes intimacy with God and your spouse difficult. In the parable of the sower, he compares our hearts to four different kinds of soil. Each of these soils is a picture of what is in our hearts that creates distance in marriage:

> Listen! A farmer went out to sow his seed. As he was scattering the seed, some fell along the path, and the birds came and ate it up. Some fell on rocky places, where it did not have much soil. It sprang up quickly, because the soil was shallow. But when the sun came up, the plants were scorched, and they withered because they had no root. Other seed fell among thorns, which grew up and choked the plants, so that they did not bear grain. Still other seed fell on good soil. It came up, grew

and produced a crop, multiplying thirty, sixty, or even a hundred times. (Mark 4:3–8)

The Hard Heart Doesn't Know How to Love

The first type of soil is a hard path. If a farmer drops grains of wheat on a highway it won't grow. The person whose heart is like the hard path is completely self-centered, so he can't respond to love from God, and doesn't know how to love others. When you have a hard heart, your relationship with God and your spouse is all about getting your own needs met.

The self-centered person feels affection for others, but not real love. You feel affection when your spouse is nice to you—if she makes you a good meal or if he brings you flowers—but real love is more than a feeling. Love means bearing in mind the interests of another person. Love is a lifelong commitment to your spouse's well-being and to building harmony and unity. If you and your spouse don't love each other like this—if you are both only committed to your own well-being—then there is a huge, distance-creating hindrance in your marriage. Your marriage won't flourish any better than a seed sown on the hard road.

The Disappointed Heart Gives Up on Love

The second kind of soil is rocky. When the seed lands, it grows quickly, but it doesn't develop deep roots, and soon the sun burns it up. This describes the heart that accepts the message of God's love in Jesus with an initial burst of enthusiasm. But when troubles come and life stops being easy and fun, the enthusiasm wanes. Your love for God was strong during the good times, but you didn't sign up for trouble. When troubles appear, you are filled with disappointment and your love for God disappears.

The same thing can happen in a marriage. When trouble comes to your marriage—your spouse isn't perfect and your life together isn't perfect either—your love wilts away. Romance is replaced by disappointment with life and each other. You may think, *I just don't love my spouse anymore.* Our culture accepts that at face value, but God doesn't. He has a different way of looking at your disappointment. God says, "You're discovering for the first time that you don't know how to love. You enjoyed affection and romance, but love is hard and hard-won. Romance is a wonderful gift, but love endures through the hard times; it endures when the heat comes."

The Distracted Heart Is Too Busy to Love

The seed planted in the third soil grows into a plant, but then it's choked by thorns. Faith in Christ can also be choked not by actual thorns, but by "the worries of this life, the deceitfulness of wealth and the desires for other things" (Mark 4:19). These are the same things that can distract you from your spouse. When worries grab all of your attention, they choke the vitality out of your marriage. A preoccupation with material things will also choke your marriage—your life together can become all about managing what you own or getting new stuff. Or your desires (your career, exercise, food, hobbies, etc.) can so preoccupy you that you have no time or energy for your spouse. You are too busy to love your spouse.

The Fruitful Heart Perseveres in Love

The fourth soil produces good fruit. This soil stands for the good heart that understands God's Word, applies it, and perseveres in loving God and others. The person with the fruitful heart has an intimate relationship with God, and she relies on that relationship for the power and perseverance she needs to love for the long haul.

What's the Condition of Your Heart?

Take a moment and assess your own heart. Do you and your spouse have hard hearts? Disappointed hearts? Distracted hearts? Perhaps all these things are creating distance in your marriage. Don't be discouraged. These are everyday human failings. You and your spouse's self-centeredness, disappointments, and distractions point to your need for redemption. You need a Redeemer to change your heart, so you can love God and your spouse.

The First-Things-First Principle

Don't make your goal in life to have a good marriage. Instead, make knowing your Redeemer your goal. Only he can teach you to love. Only he can change your heart towards your spouse. Jesus said, "For the pagans run after all these things [things like intimacy and closeness

David Powlison

in their marriage], and your heavenly Father knows that you need them. But seek first his kingdom and his righteousness, and all these things will be given to you as well" (Matthew 6:32–33). People all around the world eagerly seek to feel close to other human beings. They want intimacy. But when you seek God these "other things" will be added to you. Seek intimacy with God and intimacy with others will be added to you.

How do you seek intimacy with God? Meditate on the way he treats you. Love for others will come as you experience the love of your Father in heaven. God's love for us is the most wonderful thing in this world—it's at the core of what makes life bright and hopeful. Read these Bible verses and make them your own:

- You are never out of sight or out of mind to God (Psalm 139:7–10).
- He creates intimacy with you by the way he treats you (Isaiah 42:3).
- He notices and cares about everything that happens to you (Luke 12:6–7).
- He speaks openly about himself (John 15:15).
- He listens to you (Psalm 6:8–9).

- He is a refuge in the midst of your sufferings (Psalm 46).
- He hangs in there over the long haul (Isaiah 49:14–16).
- He laid down his life for you (John 3:16; Romans 5:6–8).
- He forgives all of your sins (Psalm 103:1–5).
- His mercies are new every morning (Lamentations 3:21–24).

God wants you to respond to his love by trusting him with your whole life. He has bridged the distance between you and him through the life, death, and resurrection of his Son. Now he is making you like him and walking with you every step of the way. He's helping you step-by-step to love others the way he loves you.

Examine your own heart to see if you are making intimacy in your marriage the most important thing in your life. There is joy and delight when there's affection, closeness, sparkle, romance, and sexual intimacy. But if you are living for intimacy, if you must have it or else, then you are not living for God.

If you are living for intimacy and you aren't getting that from your husband, you will be tempted to bitterness, despair, and even fantasizing about other men. This is where you need God's forgiveness and power to change. Center your life on intimacy with God, and he will give you the freedom to love your spouse without demanding intimacy from him.

If you seek intimacy with your spouse, you'll always be disappointed. If you seek to love your spouse the way God loves you, you'll never be disappointed. You will fail. You'll still be hurt by your spouse's sins. You'll still get preoccupied by other desires. But in the long run there will be change. Intimacy will come your way—not always the way you'd like it or at the exact time you'd like it—but learning to love God will change your relationship with your spouse.

Share God's Steadfast Love and Faithfulness

In the Old Testament two Hebrew words are often used to describe God: *chesed* and *emet*. *Chesed* is translated in the Old Testament as "lovingkindness," or "steadfast love." It means committed kindness, a chosen generosity, a resolution to do good to another person no matter what. *Emet* is translated as "faithfulness" or "truth." When we say of someone, "She was a true friend," we're using the word "true" in the sense that the Bible uses the word *emet*. It's someone who's looking out for your well-being, who is genuinely concerned for your welfare (Philippians 2:20). God is full of *chesed* and *emet*—steadfast love and faithfulness—toward you.

Chesed and *emet* are also used in the Bible to describe human relationships. Most people seek their own interests, and instinctively do things that create distance and destroy intimacy in their marriage. But when you are committed to treat someone with kindness, when you are genuinely concerned for someone else's welfare, you will start to be and do the kinds of things that actually build trust, intimacy, and companionship. *Chesed* and *emet* are what God is fundamentally like towards us. He is a God who keeps his promises, a God of kindness, a God who forgives. And *chesed* and *emet* are also the attributes you need to make your marriage deeply joyous and intimate.

Practical Strategies for Change

Now you know some of the things that get in the way of intimacy in your marriage. And you know that, as you seek God first, he will make you like himself—kind and faithful. But what does this mean practically?

Turn to God for Forgiveness and Mercy

Start with an honest assessment of your heart, so you know what is getting in the way of intimacy with God and your spouse. Are you lazy? Preoccupied? Filled with resentment? Fearful of being hurt? Finding out why there is distance in your relationship is crucial so you can know where you need to repent and where you need God's help.

The apostle Paul says that "this all-surpassing power is from God and not from us" (2 Corinthians 4:7). Ask yourself: Where do I need the surpassing power of God? Remember: *The start of change in any profound area of life is always change with respect to God.* Change begins when you recognize your need for the mercy, power, and love that you don't have. You need Jesus to forgive you. You need him to empower you. You need him to transform you into his image. You need his mercy and help to put on a lifestyle of lovingkindness and faithfulness. The power to choose your spouse's welfare over your own comes as you ask God for mercy and help.

So turn to God for help. This is the God who pursues you in love. This is the God who has *chesed* and *emet*. If you seek him, you will find him. If you ask, you will receive. Say to God, "Lord, I realize I've simply been lazy in my marriage. I've allowed myself to get too busy and preoccupied at work." If you confess your failures to God, you will experience his powerful, pursuing love. He will actually widen your conviction of sin. But you will see that where sin abounds, grace super-abounds. Your confession of sin will be the beginning of learning how to love your wife well.

Ask Your Spouse for Forgiveness

Go to your spouse and ask for forgiveness. Tell your spouse the truth about yourself. Say: "I have been distant," or "I have nursed a grievance," or "I have led a double life." Sometimes you know there's distance, but it's hard to put your finger on it. Ask your spouse this wonderfully honest, humble question (which is much easier to read than to do), "What change in me would make the biggest difference for you?" And strap on your seat belt against your defensiveness! If you react defensively, you are simply proving your pride. Hear out the answer without defending yourself.

Enter into Your Spouse's World

As you think about rebuilding your relationship with your spouse, aim to love your spouse the same way God loves you. He entered your world by sending his Son. Look for ways you can enter into your spouse's world. Start by saying, "You know, we have to spend time together. We've had lots of good intentions, but now let's actually pick a time—dinner, a walk, a cup of coffee every morning." You need to physically stop and notice each other. Whether it was five or fifty years ago, you made commitments to each other. You promised to love each other. In a distant marriage, people live on parallel tracks. You need to take the time to hold your spouse in your mind. It's easy to careen through your busy life, accumulating hurts and resentments. You need to stop and find places where you and your spouse can reconnect.

Ask Three Questions

Once you've entered into your spouse's world, ask these three questions:

1. *What are your burdens?* Get at this question by picking several of these related questions to ask your spouse.
    - What are your cares?
    - What things happened today that weigh on you?
    - What things happened yesterday that trouble you?
    - What things are you thinking about tomorrow or next week or 10 years from now that prey on you?
    - What was your low light today?

- What was the worst thing that happened to you today?

When you ask these questions and listen closely to the answers, you will find out the most amazing things. You will find out who your spouse really is. You will find out where she struggles, where you need to weep with those who weep, where you can bear her burdens, where you can encourage, and how you can pray for each other. When two people speak honestly about their burdens, they come to a deeper understanding and love for one another. This is intimate stuff, the fine china of your spouse's life. So be careful. Don't use what you hear as ammunition in an ongoing war. Instead listen, love, and pray.

2. *What are your joys?* Here's another family of questions to ask your spouse:
    - What was the best thing that happened to you today?
    - Was there a moment that brought you pleasure?
    - What are you grateful for?
    - What was your highlight today?

- As you look back over your life, as you look over the past week, what brought you joy?
- What are you looking forward to in the future?

When my wife and I ask each other these questions, we always find out something new. Sometimes it's the smallest thing, like the way the sun slanted across a cloud. Sometimes it's a positive interaction with someone that got lost in the shuffle of the day. As you share your joys, you find places where you can give thanks and where you can rejoice together. Not only do we weep with those who weep, but we rejoice with those who rejoice. When two human beings know each other and are known by each other, stuff happens relationally that it's worth weeping about and worth rejoicing over.

3. *What's your purpose?* The first two questions are about your experiences; this is an action question. Ask your spouse:
    - What's on your mind?
    - What are your goals?
    - What's going on today?

- What's happening tomorrow?
- What do you hope to accomplish this week? This year?

These are questions that get at the meaning of your spouse's life. The answer can be as small as a responsibility at work or something your spouse hopes to do with one of your children. It can be as significant as spreading the kingdom of God to the ends of the earth.

What happens when you start asking and answering these three simple questions? You start to talk about what's really happening—your joys, your burdens, and your direction. I guarantee you that those conversations will bring about the conditions that make two people one. When two people sorrow together, rejoice together, and join together in a life task, the result is intimacy and closeness.

Perhaps, as you read this, you are painfully aware that you don't have these kinds of conversations in your marriage. Perhaps your spouse has no interest in having this kind of conversation. If that is true, instead of starting with questions, start sharing your own answers to these questions.

What if at dinner you said, "Something happened today that was wonderful. I saw the first robin. And then there were 500 robins all in the tree. It was spectacular"? Or try sharing your troubles: "You know, I realized I was grumbling today when I was talking to my friend. I wish I wasn't like that." Your spouse may think you've lost your marbles, but you have moved toward him and shared yourself and your world. Just as God is in it for the long haul with you, so you are called to persevere in your relationship with your spouse. Your spouse might get uncomfortable or he might attack you, but by sharing your heart you are bringing light into a dark place and life into a dead relationship.

Express Your Love in Small, Daily Kindnesses

Love is shown in very small things. Small kindnesses tell your spouse that he is not out-of-sight-out-of-mind. Start by committing yourself to one small kindness every day. Perhaps you could pick up after yourself, just to make your wife happy. Or make a meal your husband loves. If you think about it, you probably know just what to do that would tell your spouse that you are thinking about her. If you don't know, just ask. But don't do these things to be noticed or thanked. Think of this work as a long-term investment in your relationship.

Keep expressing your love in concrete ways even if your spouse rejects you. When the apostle Paul talks about how to love your enemy, he never mentions a nice conversation. He mentions actions: a glass of cold water (Romans 12:20). If your spouse acts like your enemy, treat him the way God says you should treat your enemy. Make his favorite meal, pick up her clothes at the dry cleaners, do the small things that will make his life easier. Your spouse might hate you for doing this, take you for granted, or think you're being manipulative. But it's the right thing to do before God and, in the long run, might have a surprising impact on your relationship.

Engage in Constructive Confrontation

As you persevere in knowing God, in repentance, in constructive conversations, in kindness, there might be also a time for constructive confrontation with your spouse. You can, in love, challenge your spouse about the distance between you. You don't have to be nasty. You could say something like, "You know I value our marriage. I want us to be close, but we have been like two ships passing in the night. What can we do to be closer?" Or, "I feel like your work has been your mistress. I don't think you're having an affair with a real person, but your work has been completely capturing all your thoughts. You don't seem to be thinking about us or about me."

If your spouse doesn't respond, then you're back to the perseverance of love. If you're not ruled by your desire for an intimate marriage, then you'll be hurt by the lack of closeness, but you won't be unglued by it. You will be able to persevere in loving your distant spouse because your life is fundamentally glued together by your relationship with Jesus Christ.

If you and your spouse are living separate lives, it will take time and perseverance to rebuild an intimate relationship. How could you possibly break through the walls of self-centeredness, disappointment, and distraction that separate you without daily depending on the God who loves you? When you are tempted to despair, remember how God broke down these same walls in your life by sending his own Son into your world. Remember that he hasn't left you; his Spirit is still working to break down the walls of your heart. Depend on your faithful Savior. Trust him with your life. Trust him with your marriage. Seek him first and "all these things will be given to you as well" (Matthew 6:33).

Simple, Quick, Biblical

Advice on Complicated Counseling Issues for Pastors, Counselors, and Individuals

MINIBOOK
CATEGORIES

- Personal Change
- Marriage & Parenting
- Medical & Psychiatric Issues
- Women's Issues
- Singles
- Military

USE YOURSELF | GIVE TO A FRIEND | DISPLAY IN YOUR CHURCH OR MINISTRY

New Growth Press

Go to **www.newgrowthpress.com** or call **336.378.7775** to purchase individual minibooks or the entire collection. Durable acrylic display stands are also available to house the minibook collection.